ON THESE WALLS

· · · · ·

SOUVENIR POST CARD CO. N.Y.   4259— Rotunda, Library of Congress, Washington, D

The most magnificent interior
of any building I have
ever seen — John L. D.

ON THESE WALLS

Inscriptions & Quotations in the Library of Congress

Text by John Y. Cole

**Photographs
by Carol M. Highsmith**

✦ ✦ ✦ ✦ ✦

Library of Congress, Washington, D.C.
in association with
Scala Publishers, London

2008

PAGE 1: *The names of the construction engineers and architects who built the Jefferson Building are inscribed above the commemorative arch in the Great Hall.*

PAGE 2: *A postcard written by a visitor praising the beauty of the new Jefferson Building when it opened in 1897. (Courtesy John Y. Cole)*

PAGES 4–5: *The Thomas Jefferson Building at dusk.*

PAGE 8: *Viewed here from the top of the Capitol are the three buildings of the Library of Congress: The Thomas Jefferson Building at the center, the John Adams Building behind, and, at right, the James Madison Memorial Building.*

PAGE 11: *The dazzling two-story Great Hall of the Jefferson Building. This is the view through to the Main Reading Room on the first floor, with the magnificent mosaic of Minerva on the second floor.*

This edition copyright © 2008 The Library of Congress, Washington, D.C., and Scala Publishers Limited
Text and images copyright © 2008 The Library of Congress

First published in 2008 by Scala Publishers, Northburgh House, Northburgh Street, London EC1V 0AT, United Kingdom
www.scalapublishers.com

in association with The Library of Congress
www.loc.gov

Published and distributed outside The Library of Congress in the USA and Canada by Antique Collectors' Club Limited
Eastworks, 116 Pleasant Street, Suite #60B, Easthampton, MA 01027

LIBRARY OF CONGRESS CATALOGING-IN-PUBLICATION DATA
Cole, John Young, 1940-
On these walls : inscriptions & quotations in the Library of Congress / John Y. Cole ; Carol M. Highsmith, photographer.
   p. cm.
Includes bibliographical references and index.
ISBN 978-1-85759-545-1 (alk. paper)
1. Library of Congress—Buildings. 2. Library of Congress—Pictorial works. 3. Library decoration—Washington (D.C.) 4. Architectural inscriptions—Washington (D.C.) 5. National libraries—Washington (D.C.) 6. Washington (D.C.)—Buildings, structures, etc. 7. Library architecture—Washington (D.C.) I. Highsmith, Carol M., 1946- II. Title.
   Z733.U6C59 2008
   027.573—dc22
                    2007051744

FOR THE LIBRARY OF CONGRESS:
Director of Publishing: W. Ralph Eubanks
Editors: Blaine Marshall, Evelyn Sinclair

Project Manager, Scala: Amy Pastan
Designed by Benjamin Shaykin

Printed in China
10 9 8 7 6 5 4 3 2 1

For more information about *On These Walls*, visit the Library's Web site at at www.loc.gov.

CONTENTS

INTRODUCTION

THE THREE IMPOSING BUILDINGS OF THE LIBRARY of Congress on Capitol Hill—the Thomas Jefferson Building, the John Adams Building, and the James Madison Memorial Building—are remarkable but quite different public spaces and public works of art. All located just east of the U.S. Capitol Building, each in its own way is a powerful and impressive symbol of learning and democracy and of American culture and self-confidence. The inscriptions, names, and quotations on their respective walls and ceilings express the Library's ambitious mission of collecting and sharing the wisdom of all civilizations.

The Jefferson Building (1886–1897) proudly symbolizes an optimistic era when Americans thought it possible to create a universal collection of knowledge in all fields of endeavor. Designed and built in leaner times and primarily for functional purposes, the Adams (1930–1939) and Madison (1965–1980) buildings nevertheless employ the words and symbols of history—particularly the words of the American founding fathers—to inspire and educate.

The massive size and distinctive architecture of the Library's three buildings generally overpower these important and inspiring inscriptions, names, and quotations. This book will introduce visitors not only to the words and phrases on the buildings' walls, but also to their context—how the inscriptions, names, and quotations enhance the architecture, paintings, and sculptures of which they are a part.

Moreover, this book features new color photographs by the distinguished photographer Carol M. Highsmith. While wide-ranging in scope, its coverage nonetheless is limited; it can highlight only a representative selection of the impressive array of words that embellish the iconography of the Library's buildings, particularly in its ebullient Jefferson Building.

The Thomas Jefferson Building opened to the public on November 1, 1897. Soon thereafter, an admiring member of the public, Joseph E. Robinson, wrote the Librarian of Congress, "not until I stand before the judgment seat of God do I ever expect to see this building transcended." I hope this book will help others share at least a measure of Mr. Robinson's enthusiasm—for all three of the Library's buildings.

A BRIEF HISTORY

THE OLDEST CULTURAL INSTITUTION IN THE NATION'S capital, the Library of Congress occupies a unique place in American civilization. It was established in 1800 when the United States government moved from Philadelphia to the new capital of Washington on the Potomac River. Created as a legislative library to purchase "such books as may be necessary for the use of Congress," it slowly grew into a national institution in the nineteenth century, a product of American cultural nationalism. After World War II, it became an international resource of unparalleled dimension and the world's largest library. In its three massive structures on Capitol Hill, the Thomas Jefferson, the John Adams, and the James Madison Memorial buildings, the Library of Congress brings together the concerns of democracy, learning, and librarianship—an uncommon combination, but one that has greatly benefited American government, scholarship, and culture.

The history of the Library of Congress is the story of the accumulation of diverse functions and collections. Its collections in all formats now contain more than 138 million items—books, newspapers, manuscripts, motion pictures, music, maps, photographs, sound recordings, and graphics—from all over the world. Universal in scope, these collections have been acquired in more than 460 languages. The Library is open to everyone over high school age and makes its collections available in twenty different reading rooms.

The Library of Congress has been shaped primarily by the philosophy and ideas of its principal founder, Thomas Jefferson, who sold his personal library of more than six thousand volumes to Congress to "recommence" its library after its destruction by fire in 1814. The individual who transformed the Library of Congress into an institution of national significance in the Jeffersonian spirit was Ainsworth Rand Spofford, a former Cincinnati bookseller and journalist who served as Librarian of Congress from 1864 to 1897. Jefferson's concept of universality guides the Library's collecting policies. Jefferson believed that "there is no subject to which a member of Congress may not have occasion to refer." His belief in the necessity for an informed citizenry in a democracy shapes the Library's determination to widely share its collections.

THE THOMAS JEFFERSON BUILDING

NTIL THE THOMAS JEFFERSON BUILDING OPENED its doors in 1897, the Library of Congress was located in various places within the U.S. Capitol building. The new building was suggested by Librarian of Congress Spofford in 1871, the year after he had successfully centralized all U.S. copyright activities at the Library, initiating a growing, annual flood of books, maps, music, and other materials into the Library's small rooms in the Capitol. The focus of Spofford's efforts for the next quarter century, the building was not authorized until 1886. Construction took place between 1889 and 1897.

The history of the building, including the names of its construction engineers and architects, is inscribed on a marble tablet above a commemorative arch at the center of the east side of the Great Hall. It lists these facts: the new structure was erected under authority of the acts of Congress of April 15, 1886, October 2, 1888, and March 2, 1889; it was built under the supervision of Brigadier General Thomas Lincoln Casey, the chief of the Army Corps of Engineers, and his assistant, civil engineer and soon-to-be building superintendent Bernard R. Green; and three architects contributed to its planning, design, and construction: John L. Smithmeyer, Paul J. Pelz, and Edward Pearce Casey.

When its doors finally opened to the public on November 1, 1897, the new Library of Congress building was an unparalleled national achievement, its 23-carat gold-plated dome capping the "largest, costliest, and safest" library building in the world. Its elaborately decorated façade and interior, for which more than forty American painters and sculptors contributed commissioned works of art, were designed to show how the United States could surpass European libraries in grandeur and devotion to classical culture. Of equal importance was the flexing of American technological and cultural muscle, both powerful elements in a new feeling of national pride.

A contemporary guidebook boasted, "America is justly proud of this gorgeous and palatial monument to its National symphony and appreciation of Literature, Science, and Art. It has been designed and executed solely by American art and American labor, and is a fitting tribute for the great thought of generations past, present, and to be." This new national Temple of the Arts immediately met with overwhelming approval from both the U.S. Congress, its patron, and the American public.

The Jefferson Building is a heroic setting for a national institution: a unique blending of art and architecture that is celebratory, inspirational, and educational. Few structures represent human aspiration in such dramatic fashion.

OPPOSITE: *The torch of the cupola of the Jefferson Building gleams in a cloudless sky.*

THE WEST FRONT EXTERIOR

The Neptune Fountain Approaching the Jefferson Building, visitors encounter what was at the time the most lavishly ornamental fountain in the country. The creation of sculptor Roland Hinton Perry, it immediately introduces classical culture as a basic theme of the Jefferson Building. The colossal figure of Neptune, the Roman god of the seas, presides over a profusion of other bronze, allegorical inhabitants of the oceans.

CENTER: *Roland Perry's sculpture features Neptune, flanked by tritons blowing conch shells.* LEFT AND RIGHT: *On either side of the god, a sea nymph rides a writhing steed.*

BELOW: The American author Nathaniel Hawthorne, modeled by Jonathan Scott Hartley, is one of nine writers and thinkers commemorated by portico busts set into circular windows in the façade of the Jefferson Building.

The Entrance Porch The main entrance to the Jefferson Building is at the top of the imposing front stairway and through an entrance porch of three symbolic arches that lead into the Library's Great Hall on the first floor. Six life-size spandrel figures leaning gracefully against the curve of each of the arches are by Bela Lyon Pratt. They represent Literature, on the north end (shown), Science, in the center, and Art, on the south. Of the two figures representing Literature, one holds a writing tablet and the other holds a book and gazes into the distance.

OPPOSITE: *The bronze door by Olin Levi Warner and Herbert Adams is* Writing. *Young women represent Truth (left) and Research (right). Research holds the torch of Knowledge and Truth, a mirror and a serpent.* BELOW: *The Art of Printing, the central bronze door of the main entrance to the Library, represents the Humanities (left) and Intellect (right).*

The Bronze Doors The three arches of the Entrance Porch end at three massive bronze doors covered with designs of rich sculptural ornament. The subjects and the sculptors are, from north to south, *Tradition*, modeled by Olin Levi Warner, with large door panels representing Imagination and Memory (not shown); *The Art of Printing*, by Frederick MacMonnies, with doors depicting Humanities and Intellect; and *Writing*, by Olin Levi Warner, which was unfinished at his death in August 1896 and was completed by Herbert Adams.

THE GREAT HALL—FIRST FLOOR

The Entrance Vestibule Entering the vestibule of the Great Hall through the bronze doors at the first-floor entrance, the visitor has a unique view of the sumptuously decorated main entrance, with its gleaming white marble arches, stucco decoration, and heavily paneled and gold-ornamented ceiling. The paired figures of Minerva, the Roman goddess of wisdom and patroness of the arts and sciences—as well as war—can be seen atop each marble pier near the ceiling, each in the natural white of the stucco. In one hand, the *Minerva of Peace* holds aloft a globe, the symbol of the universal scope of knowledge, and in her other hand a scroll. *Minerva of War* grasps a short sword in her left hand and holds aloft the torch of learning in her right. Modeled in relief on the wall between the two Minervas is a splendid white-and-gold Roman tripod, used as an electric-light standard.

The Floors The flooring in the entrance vestibule is white Italian marble, with bands and geometric patterns of brown Tennessee marble (at rear). The floor of the Great Hall features a central sunburst in yellow and red Italian marble. Incised brass inlays represent the twelve signs of the zodiac, placed between floral motifs in brass embedded in blocks of red French marble.

The Commemorative Arch The arcade at the center of the east side of the Great Hall takes the form of a triumphal arch commemorating the construction of the building. The words "Library of Congress" are inscribed in gilt letters above the arch. Immediately above is a marble tablet, flanked by two majestic eagles, inscribed with the names of the building's construction engineers and architects.

The spandrels of the arch beneath the inscriptions contain sculpted figures by Olin Levi Warner titled *The Students*. The figure on the left is a youth seeking to acquire knowledge from reading. On the right, an old man is engaged in thought.

ERECTED UNDER THE ACTS OF CONGRESS OF
APRIL 15 1886 OCTOBER 2 1888 AND MARCH 2 1889 BY
BRIG GEN THOS LINCOLN CASEY
CHIEF OF ENGINEERS U S A

BERNARD R GREEN SUPT AND ENGINEER
JOHN L SMITHMEYER ARCHITECT
PAUL J PELZ ARCHITECT
EDWARD PEARCE CASEY ARCHITECT

LIBRARY OF CONGRESS

The Staircases The two great staircases flanking the Great Hall are embellished by elaborate and varied sculptural work by Philip Martiny. At the base of each is a bronze female figure wearing classic drapery and holding a torch of knowledge. Each stair railing is decorated with a fanciful series of little boys that Martiny carved in white marble.

The cherubs in the ascending railing of each staircase represent the various occupations, habits, and pursuits of modern life. Halfway up the railing on the north side are cherubs representing *Asia* and *Europe* (below). Rising above them, more cherubs represent a musician; a physician, mortar and pestle in hand; an electrician, holding a telephone receiver at his ear; and, at the top of the railing, an astronomer with a telescope and globe. On the south side (partial view), cherubs representing *America* and *Africa* sit above a bust of George Washington. Other cherubs appear to slide down the grand staircase banister. They represent different occupations: a farmer with a sickle; a vintner dressed like Bacchus, the Roman god of wine; a hunter with a gun, hoisting the rabbit he has just shot; and a mechanic with a cogwheel and pincers.

OPPOSITE: *The view of the grand staircase with Martiny's carving also shows the bust of George Washington in a niche and one of two bronze torchbearers, lamp lifted as if to illuminate the second story.* BELOW: *A pair of cherubs decorating the buttress caps of the grand staircase represent Asia (left) and Europe. The professions depicted here range from the printer, at far left, to the astronomer at the top of the south staircase.*

ABOVE: *The pair of cherubs personifying America and Africa shows the impressive depth of the carving in the marble.* OPPOSITE: *Two graceful bronze torchbearers raise their lamps, illuminating the Great Hall in all its splendor.* FOLLOWING PAGES: *Set into the ceiling, two stories (seventy-five feet) above the floor in front of the Commemorative Arch is an ornate, six-paneled stained-glass skylight, in a blue and yellow scale pattern.*

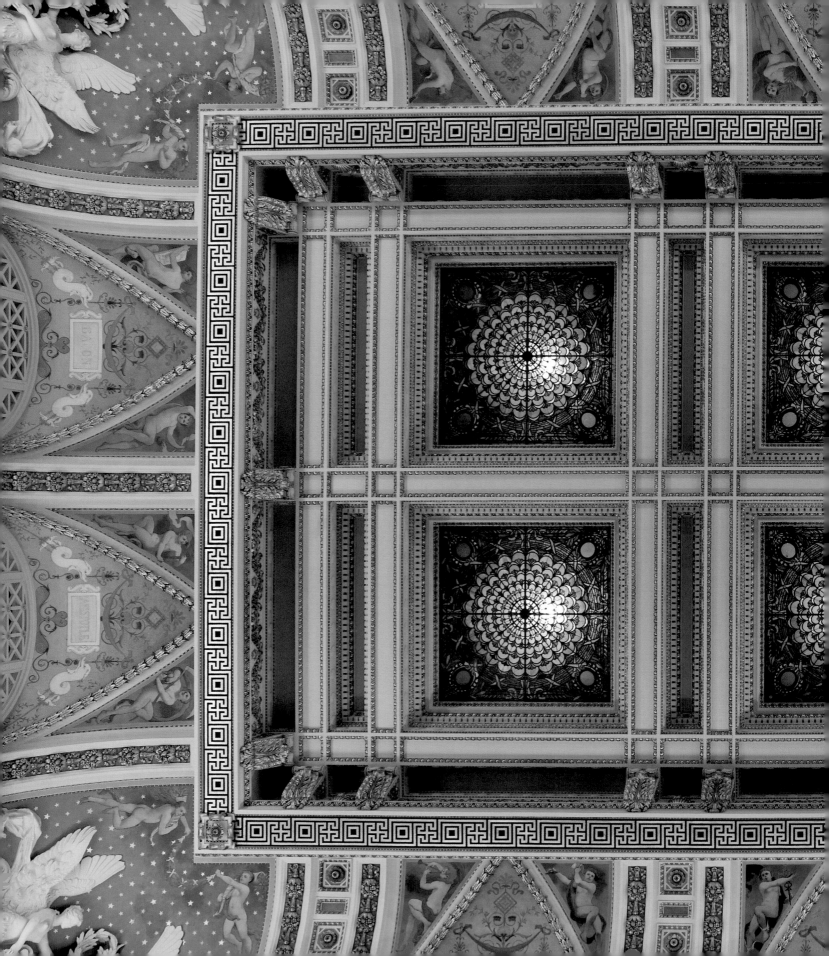

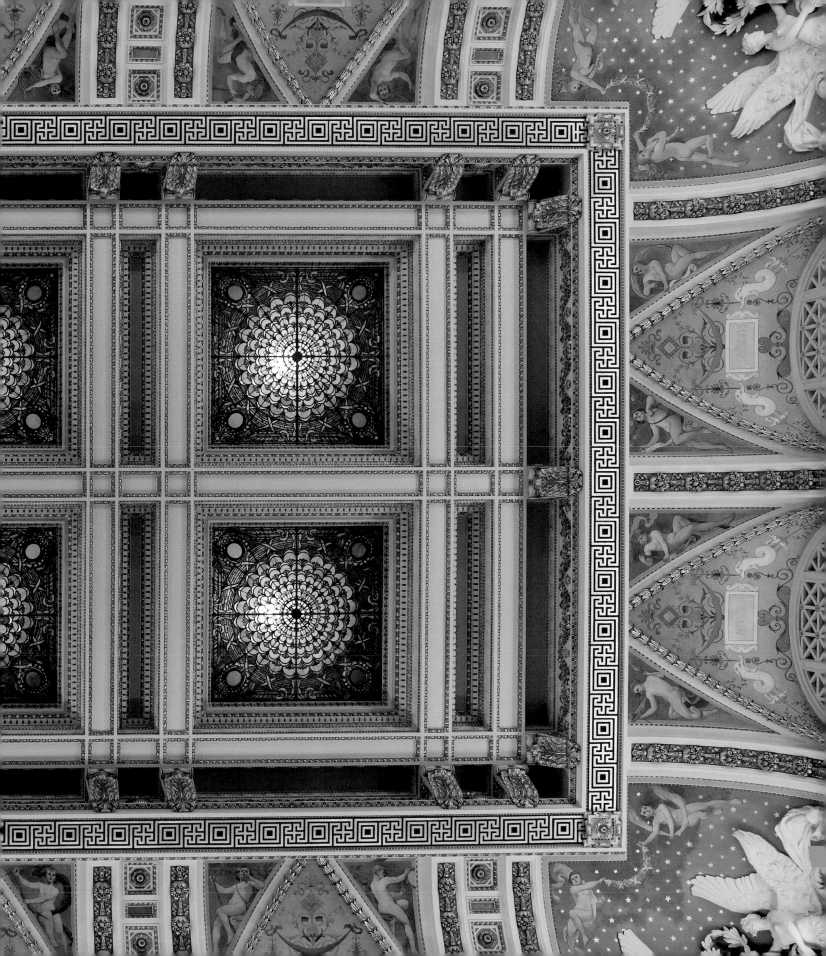

The Ceiling In its interior design and iconography, the Jefferson Building is a unique tribute to the influence of writers and their books. Librarian of Congress Spofford called it "the book palace of the American people." The surnames of ten great authors can be seen on tablets above the Great Hall's semicircular latticed windows in the vaulted cove of the ceiling. Beginning on the east and proceeding clockwise, the authors are Dante, Homer, Milton, Bacon, Aristotle, Goethe, Shakespeare (above), Molière, Moses, and Herodotus. The names of eight more writers, including three Americans, are inscribed in gilt letters on tablets beneath the second-story cartouches on the east and west sides of the hall. Beginning on the east side and moving left to right, the authors are Miguel de Savaada Cervantes, Victor Hugo, Sir Walter Scott, James Fenimore Cooper, Henry Wadsworth Longfellow, Alfred, Lord Tennyson, Edward Gibbon, and George Bancroft.

ABOVE: *Detail of the glass and plaster stained-glass ceiling, showing bands of rosettes and geometric motifs. The triangles commemorate great authors, including Shakespeare.* OPPOSITE: *Ribbons, fruits, laurel leaves, wreaths, horns, and shells carved in marble on the second floor honor the American poet Henry Wadsworth Longfellow.* FOLLOWING PAGES: *The first three of the six lunettes in the* Evolution of the Book *murals are shown beneath the lyrical mosaic ceiling in the East Corridor off the Great Hall.*

LONGFELLOW

THE EAST MOSAIC CORRIDOR

Entrance to the Main Reading Room When the Jefferson Building opened to widespread public acclaim in 1897, John White Alexander's series of six lunettes, *The Evolution of the Book*, was among the most popular attractions. The subjects, beginning at the south end, are the *Cairn*, *Oral Tradition*, and *Egyptian Hieroglyphics*; on the north side, *Picture Writing*, the *Manuscript Book*, and finally—near the Library's copy of the Gutenberg Bible—the *Printing Press*.

The lunette of the penultimate mural in The Evolution of the Book *is* The Printing Press *by John White Alexander.*

In the vault mosaics, at the ends and along the sides, ten fields of knowledge from the arts or sciences are represented by appropriate symbolic "trophies" and by the names of native-born Americans associated with that art or science: For *Law*, listed are Lemuel Shaw, Roger Brooke Taney, John Marshall, Joseph Story, John Bannister Gibson, Charles Pinckney, James Kent, Alexander Hamilton, Daniel Webster, and Benjamin Robbins Curtis. For *Medicine*, the eminent practitioners whose names appear are Samuel David Gross, George Bacon Wood, Ephraim McDowell, Benjamin Rush, and Joseph Warren.

CURTIS

WEBSTER

HAMILTON

KENT

PINCKNEY

MEDICINE

CROSS

WOOD

MCDOWELL

RVSH

WARREN

OPPOSITE TOP: *"Knowledge Is Power" is the motto of a lunette mosaic in the north lobby of the East Corridor.* OPPOSITE BOTTOM: *"E pluribus unum" is the aphorism on the mosaic lunette on the south side.* BELOW: *Elihu Vedder's Government series of five lunettes includes* Peace and Prosperity *(below), with a goddess holding olive wreaths, flanked by youths representing the arts (left) and agriculture.* FOLLOWING PAGES: *In the painting above the central door to the Reading Room, titled* Government *and representing the ideal state, one can see the figure of Good Government holding a plaque on which is inscribed a quotation from Abraham Lincoln's Gettysburg Address: "A government of the people, by the people, for the people."*

At each end of the East Corridor, a stairway leads to the ground floor. In the domed lobbies at the head of each stairway are quotations that reflect the basic themes of the importance of democracy: in the north lobby, "Knowledge Is Power," from Sir Francis Bacon, and, on the south side, *"E Pluribus Unum"*(Out of many, one), from Horace.

Five small but stunning paintings by Elihu Vedder grace the lunettes at the entrance to the Main Reading Room. This strategically placed series and its subject, *Government*, highlight the importance of learning and the spread of knowledge to the citizens of a democracy.

On either side of the central painting, titled simply *Government*, are paintings describing the practical workings of government, for both good and ill. On one side, *Corrupt Legislation* leads to *Anarchy* and on the other, *Good Administration* leads to *Peace and Prosperity*. Here, to the left of a woman holding olive wreaths that signal excellence, is a youth representing art. He decorates a piece of pottery, a lyre and small temple visible behind him. The youth opposite, who represents agriculture, plants a sapling.

A GOVERNMENT
OF THE PEOPLE
BY THE PEOPLE
FOR THE PEOPLE

GOVERN

ELIHU VEDDER
ROMA.1896

THE MAIN READING ROOM

Knowledge and Its Heroes: Twenty-four Statues From the Visitors' Gallery, eight large white statues can be seen above the giant marble columns that surround the reading room. They represent eight categories of knowledge, each considered symbolic of civilized life and thought: *Philosophy*, *Art*, *History*, *Commerce*, *Religion*, *Science*, *Law*, and *Poetry*. Beneath them sixteen bronze statues set along the balustrade of the galleries represent men renowned for their accomplishments. The bronze statues are paired, each pair flanking one of the eight large plaster statues. The name of each bronze figure is inscribed on the wall directly behind it. On large tablets high above each symbolic statue, are inscriptions appropriate to the subject. Sixteen different sculptors were responsible for these twenty-four statues.

The magnificent Main Reading Room with its massive piers. Engaged columns supporting arches create eight bays, each with a marble screen.

John Flanagan's Clock The ornamentation surrounding the great clock over the entrance to the Main Reading Room—the work of John Flanagan, who also designed the clock itself—was described by Herbert Small in his 1897 guide to the building as "one of the most sumptuous and magnificent pieces of decoration in the library."

Against a gold mosaic of zodiac signs, a life-size bronze of Father Time clutching his scythe appears to float above the clock in the Main Reading Room. Figures of women and children representing the seasons hover at the right and left, and two young men engaged in reading and contemplation lean against the clock. Below the clockface is Flanagan's bronze bas-relief *Swift Runners*.

THE THOMAS JEFFERSON BUILDING • 45

OPPOSITE: *Sixteen bronze statues of illustrious men representing various fields of thought are set along the balustrade of the galleries of the Main Reading Room. Beethoven by Theodore Baur represents Art.* ABOVE: *Joseph Henry by Herbert Adams represents Science.* FOLLOWING PAGES (LEFT): *The tablet above Philosophy is supported by two young angels. The inscription by Bacon reads, "The Inquiry, Knowledge, and Belief of Truth Is the Sovereign Good of Human Nature."* FOLLOWING PAGES (RIGHT): *The symbolic statue of Philosophy by Bela Lyon Pratt holds a book in her left hand and her mantle in her right hand. Above her head is a wreath with an open book from which hangs the lamp of knowledge.*

THE INQVIRY, KNOWLEDGE
AND BELIEF OF TRVTH
IS THE SOVEREIGN GOOD
OF HVMAN NATVRE.
BACON.

THE INQVIRY, KNOWLEDGE,
AND BELIEF OF TRVTH
IS THE SOVEREIGN GOOD
OF HVMAN NATVRE

PHILOSOPHY

The State Seals The seals of the states of the Union at the time
the Jefferson Building was constructed are reproduced in the
massive semicircular stained-glass windows that surround the
Main Reading Room. At the top, in the middle of each of the eight
windows, is the Great Seal of the United States. To the right and
the left, following the curve of each window, are the seals of the
states and territories, three on a side, six in each window. Forty-
eight seals, missing only Hawaii and Alaska, are thus included.

The name of the state or territory is inscribed above each seal,
along with the date of the year in which it was admitted to the
Union or organized under a territorial form of government. The
series begins chronologically in the west window.

THE HEAVENS DECLARE
THE GLORY OF GOD,
AND THE FIRMAMENT
SHOWETH HIS HANDIWORK

MOSES   NEWTON   SCIENCE

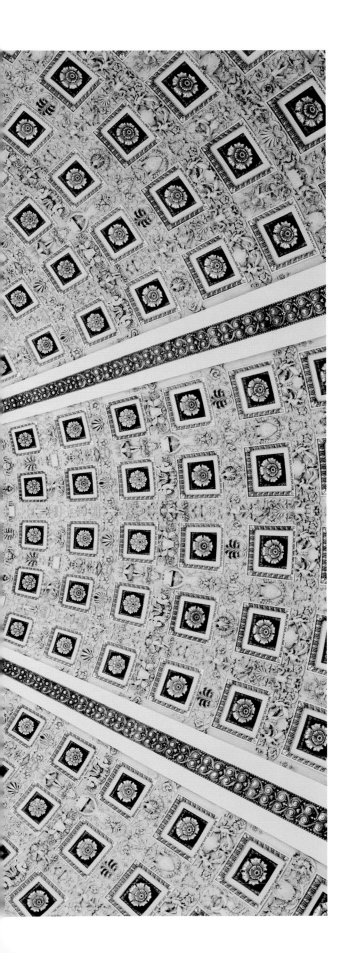

The Jefferson Building's great dome's ornate interior soars above the Main Reading Room, ringed by the large collar and culminating in the mural Human Understanding *in the oculus.* FOLLOWING PAGES: *A detail from the large collar of the dome* The Evolution of Civilization *by Edwin Blashfield, with the figure (resembling Abraham Lincoln) of America at left, associated with Science. Egypt at right represents the written record.*

The Paintings in the Dome Edwin Howland Blashfield's murals, which adorn the inner dome of the Main Reading Room, occupy the central and highest point of the Jefferson Building and crown the entire interior decorative scheme. The round mural set inside the lantern of the dome represents Human Understanding, who lifts her veil upward. The twelve figures in the collar of the dome represent countries, or epochs, which Blashfield felt contributed most to American civilization. To the immediate right of each figure is a tablet inscribed with the name of the country and, below this, the contribution that country made to human progress.

The figures follow each other in chronological order, beginning in the east, the cradle of civilization, representing *Egypt, Judea, Greece, Rome, Islam,* the *Middle Ages, Italy, Germany, Spain, England, France,* and—the culmination—*America.*

America is represented by the field of science. The figure, an engineer whose face was modeled on that of Abraham Lincoln, sits pondering a problem. In front of him is an electric dynamo, representing the American contribution to advances in harnessing electricity.

THESE DECORATIONS
RE DESIGNED AND EXECVTED BY
DWIN HOWLAND BLASHFIELD
ASSISTED BY
ARTHVR REGINALD WILLETT
AD MDCCCLXXXXVI

AMERICA

SCIENCE

EGYPT

WRITTEN REC

Give instruction unto those who cannot procure it for themselves.
CONFUCIUS

THE NORTH CORRIDOR—FIRST FLOOR

Family and Education are the major themes in this richly decorated corridor, located behind the north staircase in the Great Hall. The corridor is dominated by seven paintings by Charles Sprague Pearce. Above the window at the west end, through which a visitor can see the U.S. Capitol, is a lunette by Pearce showing two female figures holding a scroll with a quotation from Confucius: "Give instruction unto those who cannot procure it for themselves."

Six other paintings by Pearce depict related topics. The largest, *The Family*, is at the east end. Smaller paintings along the north side depict *Religion*, *Labor*, *Study*, and *Recreation*. On the south side, near *The Family*, is *Rest*.

The surnames of distinguished men of education from throughout the world are in the ceiling. On the north side, from left to right, they are Froebel (Friedrich), Pestalozzi (Johann Philippe), Rousseau (Jean Jacques), Comenius (John Amos), and Ascham (Roger). On the south side, above the columns and arches leading to the Great Hall, they are Howe (Samuel), Gallaudet (Thomas Hopkins), Mann (Horace), Arnold (Thomas), and Spencer (Herbert).

In the mosaic vaulting of the ceiling, from west to east, are the words Art (above the quotation by Confucius), Family, Astronomy (surrounded, clockwise from the north, by Mathematics, Chemistry, Physics, and Geology), Poetry (surrounded, clockwise from the north, by Sculpture, Painting, Music, and Architecture), Education, and Science (above the painting *The Family*).

The names and dates of service of the thirteen men appointed by the President of the United States to the post of Librarian of Congress are inscribed on the east wall beneath the painting *The Family*. The Librarians listed above the line served in the Library of Congress when it was in the U.S. Capitol, before the Jefferson Building was built.

THE NORTHWEST CORRIDOR AND PAVILION—FIRST FLOOR

The Northwest Corridor looks out on the right to an interior court. Nine lunettes, one at each end of the corridor and seven along the west wall, depict the Muses and were rendered by artist Edward Simmons.

According to Greek mythology, the Muses were the goddesses of various departments of Art, Poetry, and Science. Beginning at the south end of the corridor, their names appear at the center and top of each lunette: Melpomene (Tragedy), Clio (History), Thalia (Comedy and Bucolic Poetry), Euterpe (Lyric Song), Terpsichore (Dancing), Erato (Love Poetry), Polyhymnia (Sacred Song), Urania (Astronomy), and Calliope (Epic Poetry). Quotations from Alexander Pope are beneath the lunettes.

OPPOSITE: *Polyhymnia, the goddess of sacred song. On the tablet beneath her are the words: "Say Will You Bless the Bleak Atlantic Shore and in the West Bid Athens Rise Once More."* ABOVE: *Terpsichore is the goddess of dancing. The tablet beneath her lunette reads, "Oh Heaven Born Sisters, Source of Art Who Charm the Sense or Mend the Heart."*

The Librarian's Ceremonial Office Now used primarily for ceremonial purposes, this ornate room was the office of the Librarian of Congress from 1897 until 1980, when the official office was moved to the Madison Building.

The central disc in the domed ceiling (opposite) contains a painting by Edward J. Holslag of a woman holding a scroll in her hand and accompanied by a child holding a torch. On a streamer below her is the phrase *"Litera scripta manet"* (The written word endures). Figures of Grecian girls, modeled by Albert Weinert, stand in a ring around the disc; other ornaments are gilded tablets and panels bearing an antique lamp, an owl, or a book.

There are four additional circular paintings in the corners of the dome. The inscriptions, starting over the door and moving left to right, read: *"In tenebris lux"* (In darkness, light), at right; *"Liber delectation animae"* (Books, the delight of the soul); *"Efficiunt clarum studio"* (They make it clear by study); and *"Dulce ante omnia musae"* (The Muses, above all things, delightful). Weinert's masterful plasterwork creates a room of beauty and inspiration.

LITERA SCRIPTA MANET

THE SOUTH MOSAIC CORRIDOR—FIRST FLOOR

Poetry is celebrated in the corridor behind the south staircase in the Great Hall. Henry Oliver Walker's mural *Lyric Poetry* at the east end provides the general theme. Lyric Poetry stands with a lyre in the center, with the words "Lyric Poetry" in the lunette border directly above her. Other figures, seen from left to right, are Mirth, Beauty, Passion, Pathos, Truth, and Devotion.

Walker also painted the smaller lunettes along the south and north walls. In each, he depicts a youth suggested by the work of an American or English poet. The poets represented on the south wall and the poem represented by the figure in the lunette are, from east to west: Alfred, Lord Tennyson, "Palace of Art"; John Keats, "Endymion"; William Wordsworth, lines beginning "There was a boy"; and Ralph Waldo Emerson, "Uriel." On the panels along the north wall are: John Milton, "Comus"; and William Shakespeare, "Venus and Adonis."

The mosaic of the ceiling vault contains the names of lyric poets. Six Americans are honored on the north side: Longfellow (Henry Wadsworth), Lowell (James Russell), Whittier (John Greenleaf), Bryant (William Cullen), Whitman (Walt), and Poe (Edgar Allen). Poets honored on the south side are the Europeans Heine (Heinrich), Hugo (Victor), Musset (Alfred de), Byron (George Gordon, Lord), Shelley (Percy Bysshe), and Browning (Robert). The names of ancient poets are inscribed in the center of the vault: Theocritus, Pindar, Anacreon, Sappho, Catullus (Gaius Valerius), Horace, Petrarch (Francesco), and Ronsard (Pierre de).

Above the window at the west end, a broad border encloses an idyllic summer landscape. At the top is a quotation from Wordsworth: "The poets, who on earth have made us heirs of truth and pure delight by heavenly lays."

Wordsworth's "The Boy of Winander" appears as the mural figure in one of the painted smaller lunettes.

TOP: *Henry Oliver Walker's mural* Lyric Poetry *celebrates the many forms of the art.* BOTTOM: *In a broad border at the corridor's west end are a woman and a youth with a lamb opposite two more contemplative women. The poet Wordsworth's words fill the center plaque.*

THE SOUTHWEST CORRIDOR—FIRST FLOOR

The southwest corridor—leading from the South Mosaic Corridor (Lyric Poetry) to the Southwest
Pavilion—looks out, on the left, on an interior court. The nine lunettes (one at each end of the corridor
and seven along the west wall) contain paintings by Walter McEwen that represent the Greek heroes.
Beginning over the doorway at the north end and continuing along the west wall, the paintings are *Paris*,
Jason, *Bellerophon*, *Orpheus*, *Perseus*, *Prometheus*, *Theseus*, *Achilles*, and *Hercules*. The name of each hero
can be seen at the top center of each border. Four of the paintings have quotations beneath them, two by
Alfred, Lord Tennyson, the others by Charles Kingsley and George Gordon, Lord Byron.

opposite: *A lunette painting by Walter McEwen shows Paris at the court of Sparta conversing with Menelaus, while Helen sits listening to her husband and Paris talk.* above: *Hercules is at the opposite end of the corridor facing Paris. He was sold as a slave by Mercury to Omphale, queen of Lydia. They fell in love; to please her, Hercules wore women's clothes and spun with the female slaves.*

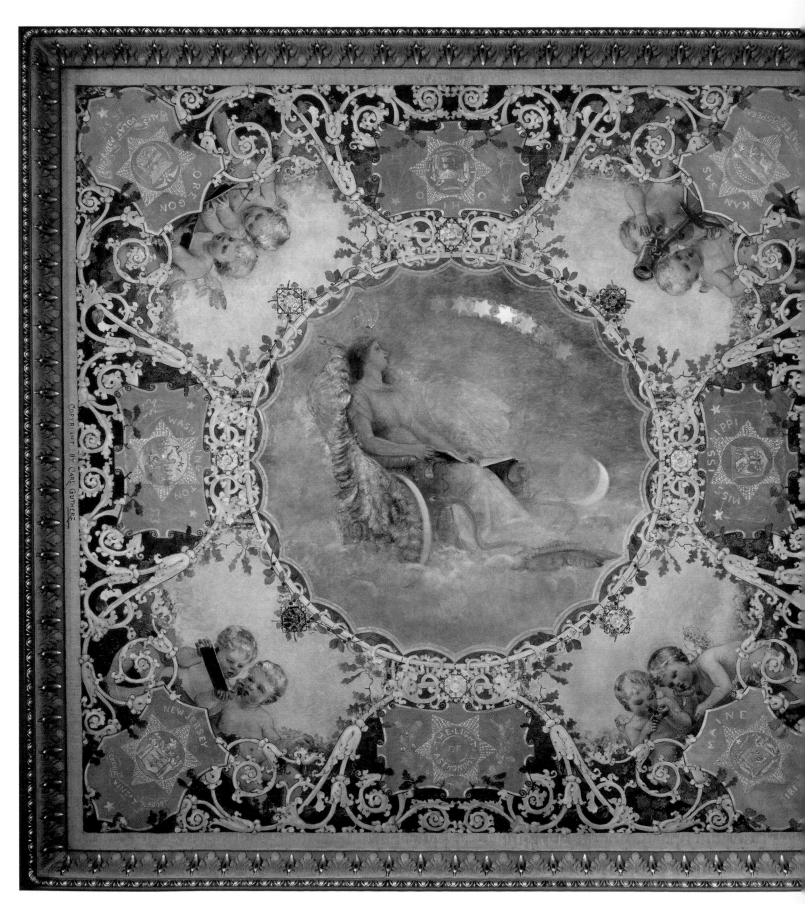

Members of Congress Reading Room Now used mostly by members of Congress and their staffs, this richly decorated gallery facing the U.S. Capitol was reserved for the House of Representatives when the building was opened in 1897. Oak doors and half-walls, decorated marble fireplaces at each end, and a paneled ceiling with seven inset paintings create a formal atmosphere.

The paintings in the ceiling by Carl Gutherz represent civilization through *The Spectrum of Light*. In the center of each of the panels is a figure who symbolizes some phase of achievement, human or divine. The cherubs in the corner of each panel represent the arts or sciences, and the escutcheons in each panel present the title of the decoration, the seals of various states, and their corresponding state mottoes. Each of the seven panels is a different color and has a different subject. From south to north, the colors and subjects are violet, *The Light of State*; red, *The Light of Poetry*; orange, *The Light of Progress*; yellow, *The Creation of Light*; green, *The Light of Research*; blue, *The Light of Truth*; and indigo, *The Light of Science*. The several hues of the spectrum are separately diffused over each panel, decreasing in intensity as they recede from the central figures.

For example, in *The Light of Science*, the northernmost panel, Science is represented by the figure of Astronomy, who is guided by the soul (the butterfly fluttering above her head) to explore the movement of the stars. The cherubs represent various phases of astronomical study, including mathematics and making calculations. State seals from New Jersey, Washington, Oregon, Ohio, Kansas, Mississippi, and Maine are depicted.

Large mosaic panels designed by Frederick Dielman are displayed over the marble fireplaces at each end of the room: *Law* at the north, *History* at the south. In the mosaic *Law*, the figures Industry, Peace, and Truth—the friends and supporters of Law—can be seen on the left side of the throne; Law's enemies—Fraud, Discord, and Violence—are on the other side. In the mosaic *History*, the predecessors of history are recognized: Mythology on the left, and Tradition on the right. On either side of the central figure are the names of great historians: Herodotus, Thucydides, Polybius, Livy, Tacitus, Baeda (Bede the Venerable), Comines (Philippe), Hume (David), Gibbon (Edward), Niebuhr (Barthold Georg), Guizot (François Pierre Guillaume), Ranke (Leopold von), Bancroft (George), and Motley (John Lothrop; the last two are the only Americans). An oak wreath symbolizes war and a laurel wreath, peace.

OPPOSITE: The Light of Science by Carl Gutherz depicts Astronomy as a young woman. ABOVE: A mosaic panel by Frederick Dielman portrays History holding a pen and a book.

SOUTHWEST PAVILION—FIRST FLOOR

The Jefferson Congressional Reading Room Now used by members of Congress and their staffs, the Southwest Pavilion was originally reserved for members of the Senate. It has been called one of the most beautiful uses of pure architectural design in the building.

The lunette over the entrance contains a carved oak panel by Herbert Adams, with a heraldic shield bearing the monograph "USA." Elegant early electric light fixtures hang from the walls, as seen below. In the southwest corner of the pavilion is a fireplace made of Siena marble, with a sculptured panel by Adams showing an American shield supported by flying cherubs (opposite).

The East Corridor In the center of the ceiling vault are three panels by William A. MacKay which represent the Life of Man, accompanied by appropriate quotations from John Milton, William Shakespeare, and an old proverb, "For a web begun God sends thread." On either side of these panels are four rectangular paintings by George Randolph Barse Jr., representing Literature. Along the east side, beginning at the north, are *Lyrica* (Lyric Poetry), *Tragedy*, *Comedy*, and *History*. On the west side, they are *Erotica* (Love Poetry), *Tradition*, *Fancy*, and *Romance*.

At the end of each ceiling vault is a tablet containing the names of eminent American printers and others who have contributed to the improvement of American printing machinery. At the north end those named are Samuel Green, Stephen Daye, Benjamin Franklin, Isaiah Thomas, and William Bradford; at the south, they are George Clymer, Isaac Adams, George Gordon, Robert Hoe, and David Bruce.

The quotations on the gilt wall tablets above the windows along the east side are from Herbert Spencer, John Keats (north side, facing the north staircase: "Beauty is Truth, Truth Beauty,") Edward Young (south side, facing the staircase: "Too Low They Build Who Build Beneath the Stars"), and from Novalis (pseudonym for Friedrich von Hardenburg).

Printer's marks, or trademarks from printers and publishers, embellish the upper walls of all four corridors on the second floor of the Great Hall. In the east corridor, these marks can be found: along the north wall, L. De Giunta, and Aldus Manutius; along the east wall, beginning on the left: P. & A. Meietos, G. Di Legnano, J. Rosenbach, A. Torresano, and V. Fernandez; along the south wall: C. Plantin and I. Elzevir; along the west wall, beginning on the left: Fratres de Sabio, Melchoir Sessa, O. Scotto, Giam. Rizzardi, and F. De Ginuta.

OPPOSITE: In the East Corridor on the second floor are four pendentive panels by George Randolph Barse Jr., representing Literature. Tradition is placed with her sisters Erotica, Fancy, and Romance on the west side. She holds a statue of the winged goddess of victory in her left arm.

TRADITION

COPYRIGHT BY
BARSE JR
1896

The Entrance to the Visitors' Gallery, Main Reading Room
The vaulting in the passageway leading to the Visitors' Gallery consists of a series of six small domes. In the medallions are various objects symbolizing the Fine Arts, Sculpture, and Architecture, accompanied by appropriate names. The sculptures are the *Farnese Bull*, the *Laocoon*, the *Niobe*, and the *Parthenon* pediment. In the bordering arabesques are the names of the four divinities often taken as the subject of ancient statuary: Venus, Apollo, Hercules, and Zeus. For architecture, iconic buildings are commemorated: the *Colosseum*, the *Taj Mahal*, the *Parthenon*, and the *Pyramids*.

Minerva, Protector of Civilization A marble mosaic of Minerva by Elihu Vedder dominates the staircase landing that leads to the Visitors' Gallery overlooking the Main Reading Room. Her armor partially laid aside, this *Minerva of Peace* is a vigilant guardian of civilization.

Beneath the mosaic is this inscription from Horace: *"Nil invita Minerva quae monumentum aere perennius exegit"* (Not unwilling, Minerva raises a monument more lasting than bronze).

NIL INVITA MINERVA QUAE MONUMENTUM
AERE PERENNIUS EXEGIT

THE SOUTH CORRIDOR

Frank Weston Benson's paintings dominate the South Corridor ceiling and wall. In the ceiling vault, the Three Graces are depicted in octagonal panels from east to west: *Aglaia* (Husbandry), *Thalia* (Music), and *Euphrosyne* (Beauty). The subject of Benson's four circular paintings on the south wall is the Seasons, each represented by a half-length figure of a young woman. From east to west they are *Spring*, *Summer*, *Autumn*, and *Winter*. At each end of the ceiling is a rectangular panel by Frederic C. Martin painted in a style depicting ancient games, but representing the modern sports of football (east end) and baseball (west end).

At the east end, bright Pompeiian panels by George Willoughby Maynard that depict *Patriotism* and *Courage* (opposite) flank the window, just as on the west end he has portrayed *Prudence* and *Temperance*.

Quotations on the gilt tablets are from John Milton, Thomas Carlyle, Sir Thomas Browne, John Russell Lowell, Ovid, Sir Philip Sidney, George Herbert, William Shakespeare, and St. John Chrysostom; and, above the west window, James Shirley.

Quotations on the wall above the golden tablets, beginning on the west end are from Alexander Pope (two quotations), Shakespeare (two quotations), Francis Bacon, William Wordsworth, and Oliver Goldsmith (two quotations). Printer's marks on the south wall, from east to west, are for Velpius, Estienne, De Colines, Regnault, Vostre, Nivelle, Morin, and Gryphe. On the north wall, from west to east, are marks for Wechel, Tory, Chaudiere, Le Rouge, Breuille, Dolet, Treschel, and Petit.

BELOW: *Pompeiian panels* Patriotism *and* Courage. OPPOSITE (LEFT): *In a tablet flanked by two square gold motifs of the lamp of learning is the quote, "The True University of These Days Is a Collection of Books." Above the circular window is a triangle holding the Velpius printer's mark. The motto is "Protect us under the shadow of thy wing."* OPPOSITE (RIGHT): *Benton's painting of* Winter *appears above a quotation from Shakespeare's* As You Like It: *"Tongues in Trees, Books in the Running Brooks, Sermons in Stones, and Good in Everything."*

CHEMISTRY

LEFT: Chemistry *is one of Walter Shirlaw's eight female pendentive figures in the vault of the West Corridor representing various scientific fields.* OPPOSITE: Archaeology *and* Botany *stand in painted arches on either side of the printer's mark for Valentin Kobian.*

THE WEST CORRIDOR—SECOND FLOOR

In the center of the ceiling vault are three panels by William B. Van Ingen representing *Painting*, *Architecture*, and *Sculpture*. On either side of these medallions are four rectangular paintings by Walter Shirlaw, representing the sciences. Along the west side, beginning at the left, are *Zoology*, *Physics*, *Mathematics*, and *Geology*. On the east are *Archaeology*, *Botany*, *Astronomy*, and *Chemistry*.

At each end of the vault is a tablet containing the names of scientists. At the north end are La Grange, Lavoisier, Rumford, and Lyell; at the south end are Cuvier, Linnaeus, Schliemann, and Copernicus. There are quotations from Francis Bacon and the Bible on either side of the south tablet, and from Ralph Waldo Emerson and Alexander Pope on either side of the north tablet.

Printer's marks along the east wall, beginning on the left, represent Cratander, Valentin Kobian, Martin Schott, Melchior Lotter, and T. & J. Rihel; along the west wall, left to right, the marks represent Wolfgang Kopfel, Fust and Schoeffer, Craft Muller, Conrad Baumgartin, and Jacob de Pfortzem.

CHARLES SCRIBNER'S SONS

WISDOM IS THE PRINCIPAL THING
THEREFORE GET WISDOM AND WITH ALL
THY GETTING GET VNDERSTANDING.

THE NORTH CORRIDOR—SECOND FLOOR

Robert Reid's brilliantly colored paintings dominate the north wall and ceiling. Reid's four circular panels on the north wall, from west to east, are titled *Wisdom*, *Understanding*, *Knowledge*, and *Philosophy*. In the ceiling vault, the octagonal decorations represent the five senses: Taste, Sight, Smell, Hearing, and Touch.

At the west end, Pompeiian panels depicting *Industry* and *Concordia* by George Maynard flank the window, just as on the east end Maynard has pictured *Fortitude* and *Justice*.

The bas-reliefs in the vault above the west window are by Roland Hinton Perry. The chief figure in each is a Sibyl or priestess—Greek, Roman, Persian, and Scandinavian—delivering a prophetic warning. Above the west window is the following quotation from Samuel Johnson: "The chief glory of every people arises from its authors."

Around the west window are five round tablets, two of which are ornamented with the obverse and reverse of the Great Seal of the United States. The other three carry quotations from Alexander Pope ("Order Is Heaven's First Law"), Cicero ("Memory Is the Treasurer and Guardian of All Things"), and Ralph Waldo Emerson ("Beauty Is the Creator of the Universe").

Quotations on the gilt wall tablets above the windows on the north wall, from west to east, are from Socrates, Alfred, Lord Tennyson, the Bible, William Shakespeare, John Milton, Francis Bacon, Thomas Carlyle, and Ralph Waldo Emerson.

Between the windows on the tablet at the east end of the corridor is this quotation from Francis Bacon: "Reading Maketh a Full Man, Confidence a Ready Man, and Writing an Exact Man."

Excerpts from a poem by Adelaide Procter are found on the seven tablets on the north and south walls. Interspersed with these quotations are medallions representing different fields of knowledge and endeavor. On the south wall, from east to west, are *Navigation*, *Mechanics*, and *Transportation*; on the north wall, from west to east, are *Geometry*, *Meterology*, and *Forestry*.

Printer's marks on the south wall, from east to west, represent William Caxton, R. Grafton, Vautrollier, John Day, W. Jaggard, Arbuthnot, A. Hester, and R. Pynson; on the north wall, from west to east, the marks are for these firms: D. Appleton and Co., the DeVinne Press, Charles Scribner's Sons, Harper Brothers, the Riverside Press, the Century Co., J.B. Lippincott Co., and Dodd Mead Co.

OPPOSITE: *Above a golden wall tablet quoting Proverbs 4:7 from the Bible is Robert Reid's painting* Wisdom, *depicting a woman holding a scroll.* BELOW LEFT: *An excerpt from "Unexpressed," a poem by Adelaide Procter, is found on the north wall.* BELOW RIGHT: *This printer's mark on the south wall is William Caxton's. Considered England's first printer, he printed* The Recuyell of the Historyes of Troye, *the first book printed in English.*

THE NORTHWEST GALLERY—SECOND FLOOR

War and Peace The paintings in the large lunettes at each end of the Northwest Gallery are by Gari Melchers and amplify *War* and *Peace*, two themes he depicted in his decorations at the World's Columbian Exposition in Chicago in 1893. At the north end, *War* shows a chieftain returning home after a successful battle; according to the artist, it was a "dearly bought" victory. On the south side, *Peace* depicts an early religious procession in a small village, perhaps in prehistoric Greece.

Names of famous generals and admirals appear on tablets above the windows and doors. Starting at the south entrance near *Peace* and moving north, they are Sheridan (Philip Henry), Grant (Ulysses S.), Sherman (William T.), Scott (Winfield), Farragut (David G.), Nelson (Horatio), William the Conqueror, Frederick the Great, Eugène (François), Marlborough (John Churchill, duke of), Wellington (Arthur W., duke of), Washington (George), Martel (Charles), Napoleon, Caesar, Alexander, Cyrus, Hannibal, Charlemagne, and Jackson (Andrew).

BELOW: *Gari Melchers's painting* War *at the north end of the Northwest Gallery shows the victorious tribal chief astride a white horse.* OPPOSITE: Peace, *at the south end of the gallery, shows a procession carrying the image of a goddess. A priest reads what may be a blessing on the fields and orchards of the villagers.*

THE NORTH GALLERY—SECOND FLOOR

In 1981 Arthur Cotton Moore & Associates was selected for the extensive restoration and renovation of the Thomas Jefferson Building. New mahogany colonnades were constructed to create reading rooms and staff offices without impinging on the historic architecture. The North Gallery became the African and Middle Eastern Reading Room.

Learning is the theme in the North Gallery. The stained-glass ceiling panels in the North Gallery contain the surnames of renowned painters, sculptors, musicians, scientists, theologians, physicians, and jurists. Designed in square panels, each section contains four inscribed tablets with the monogram "LC" in the center.

Beginning at the west end, the names listed are Holbein, Van Dyck, Rubens, Murillo; Rembrandt, Thorwaldsen, Durer, Palissy; Correggio, Titian, Raphael, Guido Reni; Perugino, Da Vinci, Apelles, Giotto; Phidias, Liszt, Bach, Wagner; Hayden, Mendelssohn, Faraday, Mozart; Agassiz, Darwin, Copernicus, Humboldt; Pliny, Euclid, Channing, Pythagoras; Edwards, Bossuet, St. Bernard, Pascal; Chrysostom, St. Augustine, Hahnemann, Bowditch; Jenner, Harvey, Avicenna, Paracelsus; Hippocrates, Marshall, Montesquieu, Story; Blackstone, Coke, Lycurgus, and Justinian.

OPPOSITE: *The African and Middle Eastern Reading Room.* RIGHT: *A feature of the adjacent northwest gallery is the stucco design in the elliptical barrel-vaulted ceilings. Here a cupid holds onto a medallion with the initials "CL" standing for "Congressional Library."*

THE NORTHWEST PAVILION— SECOND FLOOR

ABOVE: *William de Leftwich Dodge pictured Literature as a scene on the steps of a Greek temple, where the god Apollo sits holding an open book, surrounded by maidens, children, poets, and writers. A small boy at far right operates a hand printing press.* BELOW: *Music, the theme of the north lunette, is shown by Apollo, seated on a marble bench, playing a lyre, while other figures make music on a violin, trumpets, a mandolin, and double pipes.*

Ambition, *the ceiling disc in the Northwest Pavilion, reveals a dramatic and harsh vision. The rider of the winged horse grasps the palm of achievement at the top of the painting, while competitors sprawl and reach out, empty-handed, below.*

Art and Science The paintings in the four lunettes and in the ceiling of the Northwest Pavilion are by William de Leftwich Dodge. The subjects in the lunettes, clockwise from the west, are Literature, Music, Science, and Art. The subject of the ceiling disc, which is especially striking in its intensity, is *Ambition*—which the artist considers the instigator of all human effort. Places connected with these topics are mentioned on wall tablets: Greece, Italy, and England (*Literature*); Venice, Berlin, Paris (*Music*); Babylon, Tyre, Carthage (*Science*); and Thebes, Athens, and Rhodes (*Art*).

THE NORTHEAST PAVILION—SECOND FLOOR

The Governmental Seals The disc in the domed ceiling, designed by Elmer Ellsworth Garnsey, shows the Great Seal of the United States surrounded by allegorical emblems and objects that represent the North, South, East, and West sections of the country. Bordering the disc is a narrow blue band inscribed with Lincoln's best-known phrase from the Gettysburg Address: "That this nation, under God, shall have a new birth of freedom; that government of the people, by the people, for the people, shall not perish from the earth."

The paintings in the pavilion's lunettes by William Brantley Van Ingen illustrate the seals of eight departments of the U.S. government: State, Treasury, Justice, Post Office, Agriculture, Interior, War, and Navy. A circular tablet within each lunette contains a quotation from one of four famous American political figures: George Washington, Daniel Webster, Thomas Jefferson, and Andrew Jackson.

BELOW: *The ceiling disc in the Northeast Pavilion contains four medallions symbolizing the four winds. Garlands, lyres (to represent the fine arts), and horns of plenty (for agriculture) complete Garnsey's design.*

OPPOSITE: *In the ceiling disc is Maynard's painting of virtues beneficial to a developing nation.* BELOW: *"Conquest" is written at the base of Maynard's lunette painting.* BOTTOM: *Bela Lyon Pratt sculpted the plaques representing Summer and Autumn.*

The Discoverers The paintings in the lunettes and the ceiling disc are the work of George Willoughby Maynard. In the lunettes, the sequence of subjects begins on the east side and continues to the right: *Adventure, Discovery, Conquest,* and *Civilization.* In the ceiling disc, the artist has depicted four qualities appropriate to these four stages of a country's development: *Courage, Valor, Fortitude,* and *Achievement.*

The paintings in the lunettes list the names of illustrious discoverers and adventurers. In the west lunette, *Conquest,* for example, the names of Pizarro, Alvarado Almagro, Hutten, Frontenac, De Soto, Cortes, Standish, Winslow Phips, Velasquez, and De Leon are listed.

Beginning in the southwest corner and proceeding to the right, the wall tablets bear these words: Arts, Letters, Toleration, Spain, Enterprise, Opportunity, Fortune, Portugal, India, Eldorado, America, France, Exploration, Dominion, and Colonization.

Bela Lyon Pratt sculpted circular plaques in relief, representing *The Four Seasons,* in the four corners beneath the ceiling in this and in the other three second-floor corner pavilions, northeast, northwest, and southeast.

THE SOUTHEAST PAVILION—SECOND FLOOR

The Pavilion of the Elements The ceiling disc shows Apollo, the sun god, surrounded by the elements *Earth, Air, Fire,* and *Water.* The artist is Robert Leftwich Dodge. The signs of the zodiac around the outer edge are by Elmer E. Garnsey. Wall tablets bear the names Air: Hermes, Zeus, and Isis, on the north side; Earth: Demeter, Hera, and Dionysus, on the east side; Water: Proteus, Galatea, and Poseidon, on the south; and Fire: Hestia, Hephaestus, and Prometheus on the west.

Water, by Robert Leftwich Dodge, rises above the tablets naming Proteus, Galatea, and Poseidon above each window on the south side of the Southeast Pavilion.

THE SOUTHEAST GALLERY—SECOND FLOOR

Originally dedicated to Invention, the Southeast Gallery was converted to the Hispanic Room in 1938, a conversion that obscured the original ceiling and the names inscribed there. Funded by Archer M. Huntington, the Hispanic Room was designed by Paul Philippe Cret. The murals in the northern vestibule were painted by Brazilian artist Candido Portinari in 1941. Portinari's murals are *Discovery of the Land*, *Entry into the Forest*, *Teaching of the Indians*, and *Mining of Gold*. In the central hall on the east wall above the windows are the names of eminent Hispanic literary figures: Cervantes (Miguel de Savaada), Cuervo (Rufino), Palma (Ricardo), Goncalves Dias (Antonio), and Montalvo (Juan).

LEFT: Discovery of the Land, *by Candido Portinari, 1941.* RIGHT: Teaching of the Indians, *also by Candido Portinari.*

LIBRARY
of
CONGRESS

★ ★ ★

JOHN ADAMS
BUILDING

THE JOHN ADAMS BUILDING

I N 1928, AT THE URGING OF LIBRARIAN OF CONGRESS Herbert Putnam, Congress authorized the purchase of land directly east of the Library's main building for the construction of an annex. On June 13, 1930, $6.5 million was appropriated for the building's construction, and for a tunnel connecting it to the principal Library building. An additional appropriation, approved on June 6, 1935, brought the total authorization to more than $8 million.

The simple classical structure was intended primarily as functional and efficient bookstacks for ten million volumes that would be "encircled with work spaces." David Lynn, the Architect of the Capitol, commissioned the Washington architectural firm of Pierson & Wilson to design the building, with Alexander Buel Trowbridge as consulting architect. The contract stipulated completion by June 24, 1938, but the building was not ready for occupancy for another six months. The move of the Card Division into the structure began on December 12, and the doors of the new building opened to the public on January 3, 1939. The building is six stories above ground and contains 180 miles of shelving (compared to 104 miles in the Jefferson Building) and indeed was built to hold ten million volumes. There are twelve tiers of stacks, extending from the cellar to the fourth floor; each tier provides about thirteen acres of shelf space.

On April 13, 1976, in a ceremony at the Jefferson Memorial marking the birthday of Thomas Jefferson, President Gerald Ford signed into law the act changing the name of the Library of Congress Annex Building (temporarily, as it turned out) to the Library of Congress Thomas Jefferson Building. On June 13, 1980, the structure acquired its present name, which honors John Adams, the man of letters and second President of the United States who, on April 24, 1800, approved the law establishing the Library of Congress, and the main Library building was named the Thomas Jefferson Building.

The dignified exterior of the Adams Building is faced with white Georgia marble. The building's decorative style is widely admired for elements inspired by the Exposition des Arts Décoratifs in Paris in 1925, including the use of new materials such as acoustical block, formica, Vitrolite, and glass tubing. Decorative features and metalwork in the ground-floor lobbies and corridors and in the fifth-floor lobbies and reading rooms are worth special note.

FOLLOWING PAGES: *The John Adams Building.*

BRAHMA

CADMUS

TAHMURATH

HERMES

ITZAMNA

ODIN

QUETZALCOATL

OGMA

SEQUOYAH

The Bronze Entrance Doors The history of the written word is depicted in sculpted figures by Lee Lawrie on the bronze doors at the west (Second Street) and east (Third Street) entrances. The center doors at the west entrance contain six figures, which are repeated on the flanking doors of the east entrance. The figures are *Hermes*, the messenger of the gods; *Odin*, the Viking-Germanic god of war and creator of the Runic alphabet; *Ogma*, the Irish god who invented the Gaelic alphabet; *Itzama*, the god of the Mayans; *Quetzalcoatl*, the god of the Aztecs; and *Sequoyah*, a Cherokee Indian who invented the Cherokee syllabary.

The two flanking doors of the west entrance depict six other figures who are part of the history of the written word. The figures, repeated on the center door of the east entrance, are *Thoth*, an Egyptian god; *Ts'ang Chieh*, the Chinese patron of writing; *Nabu*, an Akkadian god; *Brahma*, the Indian God; *Cadmus*, the Greek sower of dragon's teeth; and *Tahmurath*, a hero of the ancient Persians.

OGMA

SEQUOYAH

OPPOSITE: *Six figures appear on the doors of the east entrance, including Nabu and Tahmurath.* ABOVE: *The center doors at the west entrance contain six figures, among them Ogma and Sequoyah, who invented the Cherokee system of writing.* PREVIOUS PAGES: *The bronze entrance doors on the east side of the Adams Building face Third Street, Southeast.*

The South (Independence Avenue) Doors   A sculpted stairway, complete with stylized owls and elaborate lamps, leads to the southern entrance on Independence Avenue. This entrance, not currently used, was originally designed for the U.S. Copyright Office.

OPPOSITE: The south doors of the Adams Building. ABOVE: A man at left in the clothes of an artisan who represents Physical Labor stands on an architectural structure, holding a vessel. At right, a woman who represents Intellectual Labor holds a scroll, her feet resting on a winged horse.

THE GROUND OF LIBERTY IS TO BE GAINED BY INCHES • WE MUST BE CONTENTED TO SECURE WHAT WE CAN GET FROM TIME TO TIME AND ETERNALLY PRESS FORWARD FOR WHAT IS YET TO GET • IT TAKES TIME TO PERSUADE MEN TO DO EVEN WHAT IS FOR THEIR OWN GOOD.

THE EARTH BELONGS ALWAYS TO THE LIVING GENERATION · THEY MAY MANAGE IT THEN AND WHAT PROCEEDS FROM IT AS THEY PLEASE DURING THEIR USUFRUCT · THEY ARE MASTERS TOO OF THEIR OWN PERSONS AND CONSEQUENTLY MAY GOVERN THEM AS THEY PLEASE.

The South Reading Room—Jefferson Murals Murals by Ezra Winter decorate the South Reading Room. The themes for the three large murals on the east, south, and west walls are drawn from Thomas Jefferson's writings. The characters and costumes depicted are those of Jefferson's time. A portrait of Jefferson with his residence, Monticello, in the background is in the lunette above the reference desk at the north end of the room; the words in the lower right-hand corner explain that "this room is dedicated to Thomas Jefferson."

On the left half of the panel on the east wall, Jefferson's view of freedom is featured:

THE GROUND OF LIBERTY IS TO BE GAINED BY INCHES. WE MUST BE CONTENTED TO SECURE WHAT WE CAN GET FROM TIME TO TIME AND ETERNALLY PRESS FORWARD FOR WHAT IS YET TO GET. IT TAKES TIME TO PERSUADE MEN TO DO EVEN WHAT IS FOR THEIR OWN GOOD.

Jefferson's views on labor, also on the east wall, are taken from his *Notes on Virginia*:

THOSE WHO LABOR IN THE EARTH ARE THE CHOSEN PEOPLE OF GOD, IF HE EVER HAD A CHOSEN PEOPLE, WHOSE BREASTS HE HAS MADE THE PECULIAR DEPOSITS FOR SUBSTANTIAL AND GENUINE VIRTUE. IT IS THE FOCUS IN WHICH HE KEEPS ALIVE THAT SACRED FIRE WHICH OTHERWISE MIGHT NOT ESCAPE FROM THE EARTH.

On the south wall, the panel over the clock contains his expression of confidence in "the living generation."

THE EARTH BELONGS ALWAYS TO THE LIVING GENERATION. THEY MAY MANAGE IT THEN AND WHAT PROCEEDS FROM IT AS THEY PLEASE DURING THEIR USUFRUCT. THEY ARE MASTERS TOO OF THEIR OWN PERSONS AND CONSEQUENTLY MAY GOVERN THEM AS THEY PLEASE.

On the left half of the panel on the west wall, Jefferson's thoughts on education are illustrated:

EDUCATE AND INFORM THE MASS OF THE PEOPLE. ENABLE THEM TO SEE THAT IT IS THEIR INTEREST TO PRESERVE PEACE AND ORDER, AND THEY WILL PRESERVE THEM. ENLIGHTEN THE PEOPLE GENERALLY, AND TYRANNY AND OPPRESSION OF THE BODY AND MIND WILL VANISH LIKE EVIL SPIRITS AT THE DAWN OF DAY.

Finally, his views on democratic government, also on the west wall, are expressed:

THE PEOPLE OF EVERY COUNTRY ARE THE ONLY SAFE GUARDIANS OF THEIR OWN RIGHTS, AND ARE THE ONLY INSTRUMENTS WHICH CAN BE USED FOR THEIR DESTRUCTION. IT IS AN AXIOM IN MY MIND THAT OUR LIBERTY CAN NEVER BE SAFE BUT IN THE HANDS OF THE PEOPLE THEMSELVES, THAT, TOO, OF THE PEOPLE WITH A CERTAIN DEGREE OF INSTRUCTION.

OPPOSITE: *Murals decorating the South Reading Room reflect Thomas Jefferson's thoughts.* BELOW: *A portrait of Jefferson and his residence, Monticello.* ABOVE: *On the south wall, the panel over the clock contains a quotation from Jefferson.*

The North Reading Room—Chaucer Murals The murals by Ezra Winter in the North Reading Room illustrate the characters of Geoffrey Chaucer's *Canterbury Tales*. The procession of characters on the west and east walls presents the *Pilgrims* in very nearly the order Chaucer introduced them. From left to right, on the west wall, the pilgrims are the miller, in the lead, piping the band out of Southward; the host of the Tabard Inn; the knight, followed by his son, the young squire, on a white palfrey; a yeoman; the doctor of physic; Chaucer, riding with his back to the observer, as he talks to the lawyer; the clerk of Oxenford, reading the classics; the maniple; the sailor; the prioress; the nun; and three priests.

The procession continues on the east wall with the merchant, with his Flemish beaver hat and forked beard; the friar; the monk; the franklin; the wife of Bath; the parson and his brother the ploughman, riding side by side; the weaver; the dyer; the arras-maker; the carpenter; the haberdasher; the cook; the summoner; the pardoner; and, finally, the reeve.

The small rectangular painting above the clock on the north wall has the Prologue of the *Tales* as its subject, and includes a quotation from its beginning. A lunette with three musicians, on the south wall under the reference desk, inspired by the Prologue of the "Franklin's Tale," is signed and dated by the artist, like the painting on the north wall.

RIGHT: *A lunette with three musicians on the south wall inspired by the Prologue of the "Franklin's Tale," is signed and dated by Ezra Winter.* FOLLOWING PAGES: *The North Reading Room—the Chaucer Murals.* ABOVE: *The clerk of Oxenford, far left, leads these pilgrims on the west wall.* BELOW: *On the east wall, the merchant and the friar lead the procession.*

THE JAMES MADISON MEMORIAL BUILDING

IN 1957, LIBRARIAN OF CONGRESS L. QUINCY MUMFORD initiated studies for a third Library of Congress building. Congress appropriated planning funds for that structure, the James Madison Memorial Building, in 1960, and construction was approved by an act of Congress on October 10, 1965, authorizing an appropriation of $75 million. The total authorization for construction eventually was increased to nearly $131 million.

Excavation and foundation work began in June 1971, and work on the superstructure was completed in 1976. The cornerstone, inscribed with the date 1974, was laid on March 8, 1974. Dedication ceremonies were held on April 24, 1980, and the building actually opened on May 28, 1980.

The Madison Building serves both as the Library's third major structure and as this nation's official memorial to James Madison, the father of the U.S. Constitution and Bill of Rights and the fourth President of the United States.

That the Madison Building should also become a memorial to James Madison is fitting, for the institution's debt to him is considerable. In 1783, as a member of the Continental Congress, Madison became the first sponsor of the idea of a library for Congress by proposing a list of books that would be useful to legislators, an effort that preceded by seventeen years the Library's establishment. In 1815, Madison was President of the United States when the library of his close personal friend and collaborator Thomas Jefferson became the foundation of a renewed Library of Congress. Like Jefferson, Madison was a man of books and an enlightened statesman who believed the power of knowledge was essential for individual liberty and democratic government.

Modern in style, the Madison Building was designed by the firm of DeWitt, Poor, and Shelton, Associated Architects. When it opened, it was one of the three largest public buildings in Washington, D.C. (the other two were the Pentagon and the F.B.I. Building). It contains 2.1 million square feet with 1.5 million square feet used for offices, reading rooms, and special collections.

Over the main entrance is the four-story-tall bronze relief, *Falling Books*, by Frank Eliscu. Two quotations from the writings of James Madison adorn the exterior walls of the Madison Building, on either side of the main entrance on Independence Avenue. On the left side: "Knowledge will forever govern ignorance, and a people who mean to be their own governours must arm themselves with the power which knowledge gives." On the right side: "What spectacle can be more edifying or more seasonable than that of liberty & learning each leaning on the other for their mutual & surest support?"

FOLLOWING PAGES: The Madison Building is the nation's official memorial to James Madison, the fourth President of the United States, known as the father of the U.S. Constitution and Bill of Rights.

OPPOSITE: *Over the main entrance is a four-story relief in bronze, Falling Books, by Frank Eliscu.* RIGHT: *Two quotations from James Madison adorn the marble exterior walls of the building, on either side of the main entrance on Independence Avenue. On the right side is a quote from Madison that speaks of liberty and learning being dependent on one another. On the left side is a quote concerning Knowledge.*

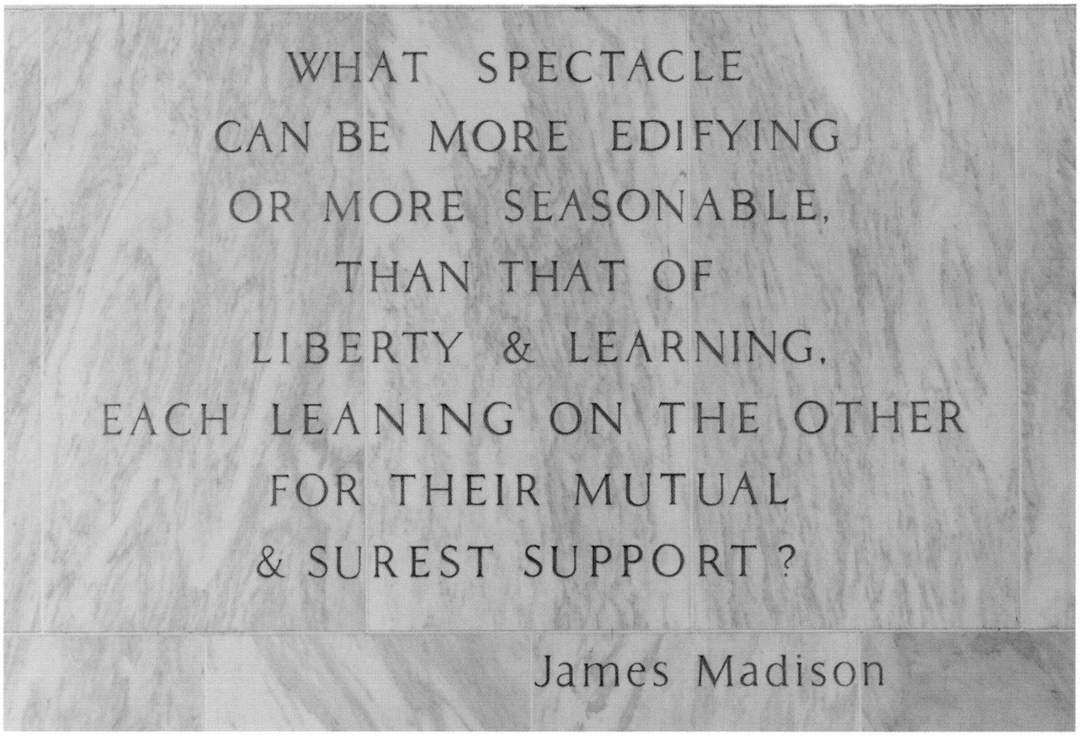

WHAT SPECTACLE
CAN BE MORE EDIFYING
OR MORE SEASONABLE,
THAN THAT OF
LIBERTY & LEARNING,
EACH LEANING ON THE OTHER
FOR THEIR MUTUAL
& SUREST SUPPORT?

James Madison

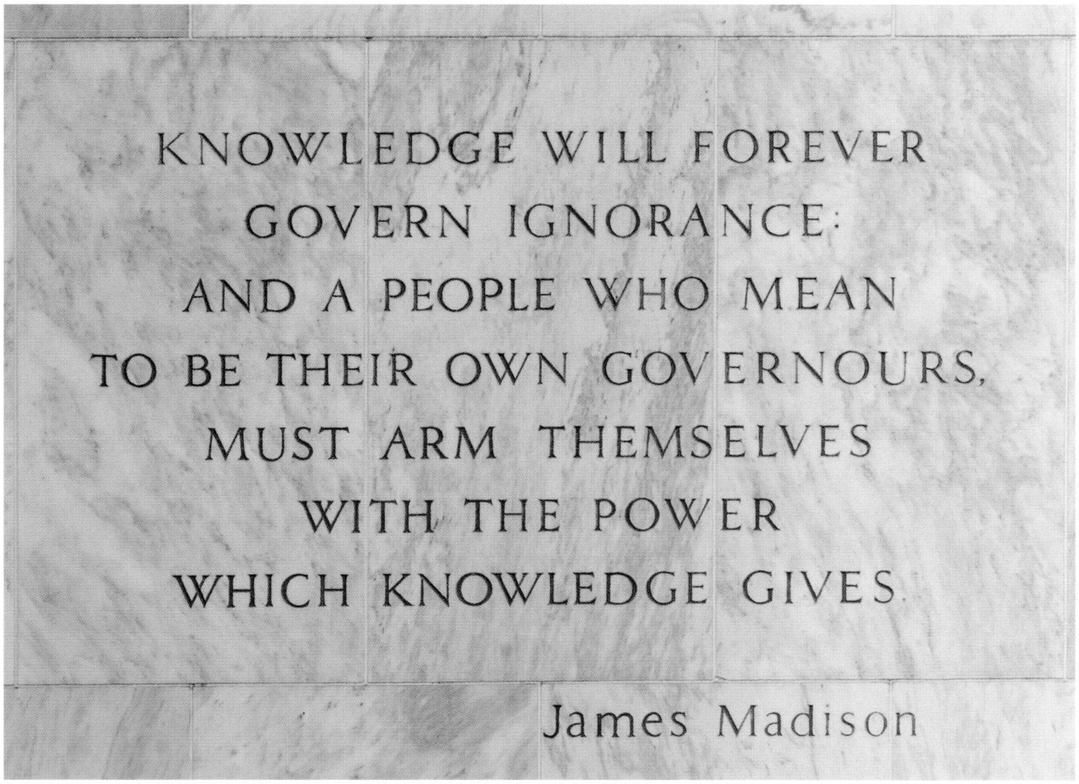

KNOWLEDGE WILL FOREVER
GOVERN IGNORANCE:
AND A PEOPLE WHO MEAN
TO BE THEIR OWN GOVERNOURS,
MUST ARM THEMSELVES
WITH THE POWER
WHICH KNOWLEDGE GIVES.

James Madison

James Madison Memorial Hall Off the entrance hall is the James Madison Memorial Hall, which features a heroic statue by Walker K. Hancock that portrays Madison as a man in his thirties, holding in his right hand volume 83 of the *Encyclopédie Méthodique*, published in Paris between 1782 and 1832.

Eight quotations from James Madison concerning government and individual rights were incised by Constantine L. Seferlis in the teakwood panels of the Madison Hall near the front entrance.

The quotations are:

LEARNED INSTITUTIONS OUGHT TO BE FAVORITE OBJECTS WITH EVERY FREE PEOPLE. THEY THROW THAT LIGHT OVER THE PUBLIC MIND WHICH IS THE BEST SECURITY AGAINST CRAFTY & DANGEROUS ENCROACHMENTS ON THE PUBLIC LIBERTY.

THE HAPPY UNION OF THESE STATES IS A WONDER; THEIR CONSTITUTION A MIRACLE; THEIR EXAMPLE THE HOPE OF LIBERTY THROUGHOUT THE WORLD.

THE ESSENCE OF GOVERNMENT IS POWER; AND POWER, LODGED AS IT MUST BE IN HUMAN HANDS, WILL EVER BE LIABLE TO ABUSE.

EQUAL LAWS PROTECTING EQUAL RIGHTS ARE . . . THE BEST GUARANTEE OF LOYALTY & LOVE OF COUNTRY.

AS A MAN IS SAID TO HAVE A RIGHT TO HIS PROPERTY, HE MAY BE EQUALLY SAID TO HAVE A PROPERTY IN HIS RIGHTS.

WAR CONTAINS MUCH FOLLY, AS WELL AS WICKEDNESS, THAT MUCH IS TO BE HOPED FROM THE PROGRESS OF REASON; AND IF ANYTHING IS TO BE HOPED, EVERYTHING OUGHT TO BE TRIED.

THE FREE SYSTEM OF GOVERNMENT WE HAVE ESTABLISHED IS SO CONGENIAL WITH REASON, WITH COMMON SENSE, AND WITH A UNIVERSAL FEELING THAT IT MUST PRODUCE APPROBATION AND A DESIRE OF IMITATION, AS AVENUES MAY BE FOUND FOR TRUTH TO THE KNOWLEDGE OF NATIONS.

THE SAFETY AND HAPPINESS OF SOCIETY ARE THE OBJECTS AT WHICH ALL POLITICAL INSTITUTIONS AIM, AND TO WHICH ALL INSTITUTIONS MUST BE SACRIFICED.

OPPOSITE: *Just inside the Madison Building and directly to the left of the entrance is the gallery of the James Madison Memorial Hall. A heroic statue by Walker K. Hancock portrays Madison as a young man in his thirties.* RIGHT: *One of the eight quotations from James Madison concerning government and individual rights that are incised in teakwood panels.*

THE HAPPY UNION
OF THESE STATES IS A WONDER:
THEIR CONSTITUTION A MIRACLE:
THEIR EXAMPLE
THE HOPE OF LIBERTY
THROUGHOUT THE WORLD.

Above the doors to the Manuscript Reading Room is a bronze medallion profile of James Madison. Another, showing Madison at his writing desk, is affixed above the entrance to the Manuscript Division offices. Both medallions are by Robert Alexander Weinman.

A large globe stands on the first floor of the Madison Building. Above the entrance of the building, the sculpture Falling Books *is visible through the window.*

*An owl, the symbol of learning and wisdom, appears often
in the Adams Building, in the ground-floor lobbies and
corridors and the fifth-floor lobbies and reading rooms.*

BIOGRAPHICAL DICTIONARY OF THE ARTISTS

THE THOMAS JEFFERSON BUILDING

Herbert Adams, 1858–1948, SCULPTOR (brass front door, *Writing*). Born in West Concord, Vermont. Studied sculpture in Boston, then in Paris under Antonin Mercié from 1885 to 1890. Did bronze doors of St. Bartholomew's Church, Hoyt Memorial in Judson Memorial Church, and statue of William Cullen Bryant in Bryant Park, all in New York.

John White Alexander, 1856–1915, PAINTER (lunettes, *The Evolution of the Book*). Born in Allegheny, Pennsylvania. At eighteen, he began illustrating for *Harper's Weekly*. In New York in 1881, he made his reputation as a leading portrait painter and was an instructor at the Art Students League.

George Randolph Barse Jr., 1861–1938, PAINTER (eight rectangular paintings representing Literature, Great Hall, second floor). Born in Detroit, Michigan. Instructor at Art Students League in New York, 1894–1896. Noted for figures and portraits.

Frank Weston Benson, 1862–1951, PAINTER (*The Three Graces*, south corridor, the Great Hall). Born in Salem, Massachusetts. Attended Boston Museum of Fine Arts School. Member of "The Ten," a group of Boston and New York artists of whom the best known was Childe Hassam.

Edwin Howland Blashfield, 1848–1936, PAINTER (collar murals and inner dome of the Main Reading Room). Born in Brooklyn, he studied in Paris under Léon Bonnat from 1867 to 1870 and from 1874 to 1880. His first mural decoration was presented at the World's Columbian Exposition of 1893 in Chicago.

Frederick Dielman, 1847–1935, PAINTER (mosaic panels, Members of Congress Reading Room). Born in Hanover, Germany. From 1866 to 1872, Dielman was a topographer and draftsman with the United States Corps of Engineers. From 1903 to 1918, he was professor of drawing at Columbia College of the City of New York and from 1903 to 1931, he was the director of the Art School of Cooper Union. President of National Academy of Design, 1900–1909.

William de Leftwich Dodge, 1872–1940, PAINTER (ceiling lunettes, Northwest Pavilion; ceiling disc, Southeast Pavilion). Born in Bedford, Virginia. Studied in Munich and Paris, in latter city under Jean Léon Gérôme. Illustrator for *Le Figaro Illustré*, *Colliers Magazine*, and other publications. Other murals can be found in the Brooklyn Academy of Music and New York State Capitol in Albany.

John Flanagan, 1865–1952, SCULPTOR (clock, Main Reading Room). Born in Newark, New Jersey. Other work includes bronze relief for the Newark, New Jersey, Public Library and Langley Memorial at the Smithsonian Institution.

Elmer Ellsworth Garnsey, 1862–1946, PAINTER (ceiling disc, Northeast Pavilion). Born in Holmden, New Jersey. Attended Cooper Union and the Art Students League, New York. Did color decoration of Boston Public Library and Carnegie Institute in Pittsburgh; also painted panels for the library of the Andrew Carnegie residence, now the Cooper-Hewitt Museum in New York.

Carl Gutherz, 1844–1907, PAINTER (ceiling paintings, Members of Congress Reading Room). Born in Aargau, Switzerland. In 1851, moved with family to Cincinnati, Ohio, and a year later to Memphis, Tennessee. Founded the art department of Washington University, St. Louis, Missouri.

Jonathan Scott Hartley, 1845–1912, SCULPTOR (busts of Emerson, Irving, and Hawthorne). Born in Albany, New York. Studied at the Art Students League, New York, Royal Academy, London, and then in Berlin, Rome, and Paris. Other work includes John Ericsson Monument in Battery Park, New York, and the Daguerre Monument in Washington.

Edward J. Holslag, 1870–1925, PAINTER (central ceiling disc, Librarian's Ceremonial Office). Born in Buffalo, New York. Holslag lived in Chicago and decorated hotels and banks around the country.

William A. MacKay, 1878–1934, PAINTER (panels representing the *Life of Man*, second floor, Great Hall). Born in Philadelphia. His other work appears in the Minnesota State Capitol in St. Paul; Essex County Courthouse in Newark, New Jersey; and large murals in the Theodore Roosevelt Memorial, American Museum of Natural History, New York.

Frederick MacMonnies, 1863–1937, SCULPTOR (bronze doors representing *The Art of Printing*). Born in Brooklyn, New York. Other work includes statues of J.S.T. Stranahan in Prospect Park, Nathan Hale in City Hall Park, and four spandrel figures for Washington Arch (1894), Washington Square Park, all in New York. Among his most important sculptural work was *Ship of State*, with twenty-seven figures, at the World's Columbian Exposition of 1893 in Chicago.

Philip Martiny, 1858–1927, SCULPTOR (putti, Great Hall staircase; bronze female figures, Great Hall staircase). Born in Strasbourg, France. Other work includes lions for the Boston Public Library and work for McKim, Mead & White's Agricultural Building at the World's Columbian Exposition of 1893.

George Willoughby Maynard, 1843–1923, PAINTER (North Corridor, panels depicting *Industry* and *Concordia*; lunettes and domed ceiling disc, Southwest Pavilion). Born in Washington, D.C. Studied at the National Academy of Design and the Art Students League, New York. Other work includes the ceiling of the auditorium of the old Metropolitan Opera House in New York.

Walker McEwen, 1860–1943, PAINTER (Southwest Corridor paintings of Greek heroes). Born in Chicago. Studied at the Royal Academy in Munich. Best known as a genre and portrait painter.

Gari Melchers, 1860–1932, PAINTER (Northwest Gallery, lunettes of *War* and *Peace*). Born in Detroit. Studied in Düsseldorf, then in Paris. Worked at World's Columbian Exposition of 1893 in Chicago. Did mural work in the Detroit Public Library.

Charles Sprague Pearce, 1851–1914, PAINTER (North Corridor, series of seven paintings). Born in Boston. Studied under Léon Bonnat in Paris. Lived most of his life in Auvers-sur-Oise, France, painting in France and Algeria.

Roland Hinton Perry, 1870–1941, SCULPTOR and PAINTER (Neptune Fountain; bas relief, South Corridor, west window). Born in New York. Studied in Paris from 1890 to 1894. Other work includes statues on the dome of the Pennsylvania State Capitol in Harrisburg.

Candido Portinari, 1903–1962, PAINTER (murals, Hispanic Reading Room). Born in Brodowski, near Sao Paulo, Brazil. Attended the School of Fine Arts in Rio de Janiero and also did murals for the United Nations.

Bela Lyon Pratt, 1867–1917, SCULPTOR (statue figure *Philosophy* and *Four Seasons*). Born in Norwich, Connecticut. Studied with Augustus Saint-Gaudens, William Merritt Chase, and Kenyon Cox in New York. Other work includes a statue of Edward Everett Hale in Boston Public Gardens; and the sculpture on the façade of the Boston Museum of Fine Arts.

Robert Reid, 1862–1929, PAINTER (paintings *Wisdom*, *Understanding*, *Knowledge*, and *Philosophy*). Born in Stockbridge, Massachusetts. Studied at the Boston Museum of Fine Arts and Art Students League of New York. Part of a group of New York and Boston Impressionists called "The Ten," the best known of whom was Childe Hassam.

Walter Shirlaw, 1838–1909, PAINTER (West Corridor, eight paintings representing the Sciences). Born in Paisley, Scotland, raised in New York. Began artistic life as an engraver, but turned to painting. Did genre and portraits as well as mural work.

Edward Simmons, 1852–1931, PAINTER (*The Muses*, Northwest Corridor). Born in Concord, Massachusetts. Graduated from Harvard (1874) and was a founder of the Harvard *Crimson*. Other work includes the South Dakota State Capitol in Bismarck; John D. Rockefeller residence in Pocantico Hills, New York; and Frederick Vanderbilt Mansion, Hyde Park, New York.

William Brantley Van Ingen, 1858–1955, PAINTER (ceiling vault paintings, West Corridor, representing *Architecture*, *Sculpture*, and *Painting*). Born in Philadelphia. Studied under Thomas Eakins in Philadelphia and under John La Farge, Francis Lathrop, and Louis Comfort Tiffany in New York. Decorated the Pennsylvania State Capitol, Harrisburg; Administration Building, Panama Canal Zone; and New York State College for Teachers in Albany.

Elihu Vedder, 1836–1923, PAINTER (five paintings, representing Government; entrance to Main Reading Room; marble mosaic *Minerva*). Born in New York. Other mural works decorate the Walker Art Gallery, Bowdoin College, Maine, and Collis P. Huntington's New York house, which became Yale University's Art Gallery.

Henry Oliver Walker, 1843–1929, PAINTER (murals and lunettes, South Mosaic Corridor, *Lyric Poetry*). Born in Boston. Studied under Léon Bonnat in Paris. His other mural work can be found in the Massachusetts State House in Boston and the Minnesota State Capitol in St. Paul.

Olin Levi Warner, 1844–1896, SCULPTOR (door panels depicting *Imagination* and *Writing*). Born in Suffield, Connecticut. Did portrait busts of Governor William A. Buckingham in the Connecticut State Capitol in Hartford and a statue of William Lloyd Garrison on Commonwealth Avenue, Boston.

Albert Weinert, 1863–1947, SCULPTOR (stucco ornamentation in Librarian's Ceremonial Office). Born in Leipzig. Attended the Royal Academy in Leipzig. Other work includes Lord Baltimore Monument, Baltimore; statue of Governor Stevens T. Mason, Detroit, Michigan; and McKinley Monument in Toledo, Ohio.

THE JOHN ADAMS BUILDING

Lee Lawrie, 1877–1963, SCULPTOR (bronze doors). Born in Rixdorf, Germany. Studied with Augustus Saint-Gaudens and Philip Martiny. Among his other works are decorations for the U.S. Military Academy at West Point and *Atlas* at Rockefeller Center, New York.

Ezra Winter, 1886–1949, MURALIST (*Canterbury Tales*, North Reading Room and Jefferson murals, South Reading Room). Born in Manistee, Michigan. He studied at the Chicago Academy of Fine Arts in 1908 and 1909. His other work can be seen in New York City at the Cunard Building, the Cotton Exchange, and Rockefeller Center.

THE JAMES MADISON MEMORIAL BUILDING

Frank Eliscu, 1912–1996, SCULPTOR (*Falling Books*). Born in Washington Heights, New York. Graduated from Pratt Institute in 1931 and from New York Teacher's College in 1942. His most famous sculpture was the Heisman Memorial Trophy.

Walker K. Hancock, 1901–1998, SCULPTOR (statue of James Madison). Born in St. Louis, Missouri. A teacher at the Pennsylvania Academy from 1929 to 1968, and a sculptor in residence at the American Academy in Rome from 1956 to 1957. A major commission was the *Pennsylvania Railroad War Memorial*, completed 1950 and located at the Thirtieth Street Station in Philadelphia.

Robert Alexander Weinman, 1915–2003, SCULPTOR (two bronze medallions of James Madison). Studied at the Art Students League and National Academy of Design, New York, and with his father, Adolph A. Weinman.

BUILDING FLOOR PLANS

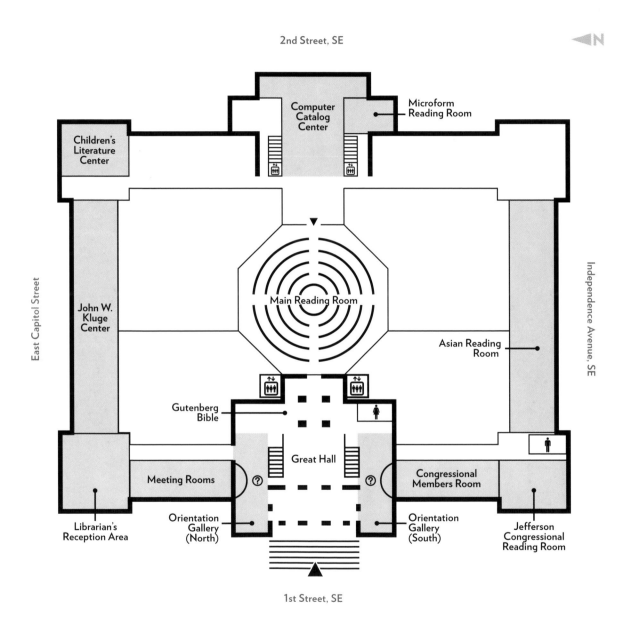

2nd Street, SE

Computer Catalog Center

Microform Reading Room

Children's Literature Center

East Capitol Street

John W. Kluge Center

Main Reading Room

Asian Reading Room

Independence Avenue, SE

Gutenberg Bible

Great Hall

Congressional Members Room

Meeting Rooms

Librarian's Reception Area

Orientation Gallery (North)

Orientation Gallery (South)

Jefferson Congressional Reading Room

1st Street, SE

THE THOMAS JEFFERSON BUILDING
FIRST FLOOR

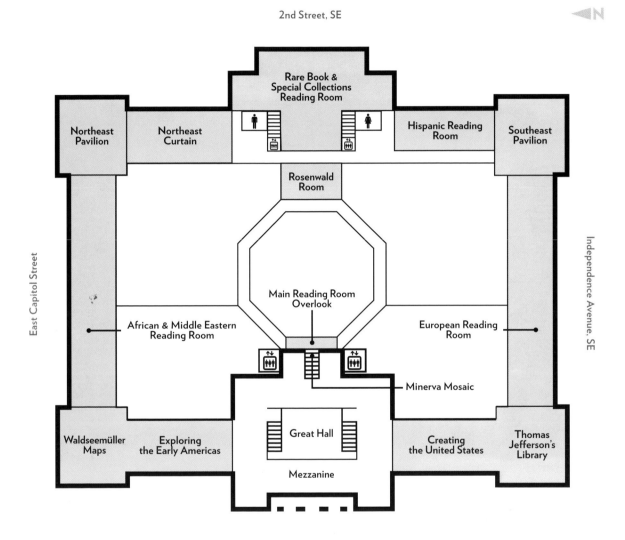

2nd Street, SE

N

Rare Book &
Special Collections
Reading Room

Northeast
Pavilion

Northeast
Curtain

Hispanic Reading
Room

Southeast
Pavilion

Rosenwald
Room

East Capitol Street

Independence Avenue, SE

Main Reading Room
Overlook

African & Middle Eastern
Reading Room

European Reading
Room

Minerva Mosaic

Great Hall

Waldseemüller
Maps

Exploring
the Early Americas

Creating
the United States

Thomas
Jefferson's
Library

Mezzanine

1st Street, SE

THE THOMAS JEFFERSON BUILDING
SECOND FLOOR

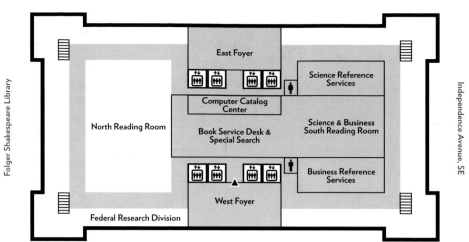

3rd Street, SE

N

Folger Shakespeare Library

East Foyer

Science Reference Services

Computer Catalog Center

North Reading Room

Book Service Desk & Special Search

Science & Business South Reading Room

Business Reference Services

Independence Avenue, SE

West Foyer

Federal Research Division

2nd Street, SE

THE JOHN ADAMS BUILDING
FIFTH FLOOR

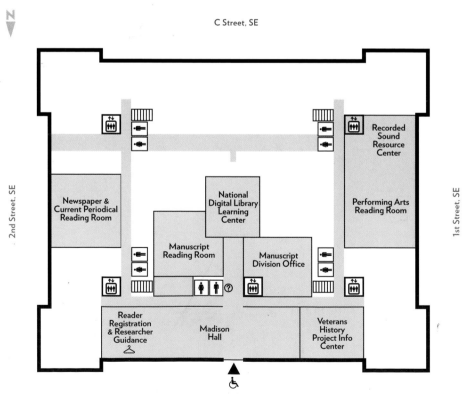

N

C Street, SE

Recorded Sound Resource Center

2nd Street, SE

Newspaper & Current Periodical Reading Room

National Digital Library Learning Center

Performing Arts Reading Room

1st Street, SE

Manuscript Reading Room

Manuscript Division Office

Reader Registration & Researcher Guidance

Madison Hall

Veterans History Project Info Center

Independence Avenue, SE

THE JAMES MADISON MEMORIAL BUILDING
FIRST FLOOR